# Cascading Style Sheets Rock star
**BOOK 2:** Techniques Every Web Developer Should Know

## Table of Contents

**Learning Objectives**

After completing this section, learners will be able to:

**A. CSS and Color Management**
- Identify different color formats in CSS, including named colors, hex codes, RGB, HSL, and currentColor.
- Apply **opacity** and **alpha channels** for transparent effects.
- Use modern color functions like color-mix() (where supported) for dynamic color blending.

**B. Working with Gradients**
- Differentiate between **linear** and **radial** gradients.
- Construct multi-color gradients using precise stops and angles.
- Apply gradients to background layers and individual elements.

**C. Using Box Shadows**
- Define **box-shadow** properties such as offset, blur radius, spread, and color.
- Apply inner and outer shadows to elements for emphasis and depth.

**D. Text Styling Essentials**
- Control **font family, size, weight, and style** using CSS typography properties.
- Apply spacing adjustments such as **line-height, letter-spacing, and word-spacing**.
- Use properties like **text-align** and **text-transform** to enhance text presentation.

**E. Applying Text Shadows**
- Define **text-shadow** properties to add depth, contrast, and emphasis to text.
- Apply multiple shadows for creative text effects.

**F. Rounded Corners and Shape Control**
- Use the **border-radius** property to create rounded corners.
- Apply different radius values for each corner to achieve custom shapes.

**G. Border Images**
- Replace standard borders with images using the **border-image** property.
- Define **slice, width, and outset** to control how images fit along borders.

**H. Multi-Background Techniques**
- Apply multiple background images, gradients, and colors to a single element.
- Control positioning, sizing, and repetition for each background layer.

**I. Box Decoration Breaks**
- Use the **box-decoration-break** property to control how decorations (like borders and background images) behave when elements split across lines, pages, or columns.

**J. Caret and Selection Styling**
- Customize the color of the **text caret** using the **caret-color** property.

- Apply styling to highlighted text using the **::selection** pseudo-element.

**K. 2D Transforms**
- Use **transform** functions such as rotate(), scale(), translate(), and skew() to adjust element positioning and appearance in 2D space.

**L. 3D Transforms**
- Apply 3D transformations using rotate3d(), translate3d(), and scale3d().
- Define **perspective** to create depth and simulate 3D space.

**M. Transitions**
- Define smooth **transitions** between element states using properties like transition-property, transition-duration, and transition-timing-function.
- Apply multiple transitions to a single element.

**N. CSS Animations**
- Create keyframe animations using the @keyframes rule.
- Apply animations using properties like animation-name, animation-duration, and animation-iteration-count.
- Combine multiple animation properties for complex sequences.

**O. Multi-Column Layouts**
- Use **columns** properties to create multi-column text layouts.
- Control **column width, column count, and column gaps**.
- Apply properties like **column-rule** and **column-span** to customize appearance.

## A. <u>CSS and Color Management</u>

Color plays a crucial role in web design, helping to create visual hierarchy, brand identity, and user-friendly interfaces. CSS provides several ways to define and manage colors, making it essential for web developers to understand the available color formats and how to apply them effectively.

**Understanding Color Values, Transparency, and Modern Color Functions**

**Color Values in CSS**

CSS supports multiple ways to define colors. The most common methods include:

| Color Value Type | Example | Description |
|---|---|---|
| Named Colors | `color: red;` | Predefined color names, such as `blue`, `green`, or `tomato`. |
| Hexadecimal | `color: #ff5733;` | Uses a # followed by 6 digits, representing red, green, and blue (RGB) values. |
| RGB | `color: rgb(255, 87, 51);` | Specifies red, green, and blue values directly (0-255 each). |
| HSL | `color: hsl(10, 100%, 60%);` | Uses hue (angle on color wheel), saturation, and lightness. |

**Transparency and Alpha Channels**

Modern designs often require transparent elements, especially for overlays or effects. CSS supports alpha channels to control transparency:

| Format | Example | Description |
|---|---|---|
| RGBA | `color: rgba(255, 87, 51, 0.5);` | Adds a 4th value (alpha), representing opacity (0 = fully transparent, 1 = fully opaque). |
| HSLA | `color: hsla(10, 100%, 60%, 0.3);` | Adds alpha to HSL colors. |

**Example**

p {

    background-color: rgba(0, 0, 0, 0.5); /* Semi-transparent black background */

}

**Modern Color Functions**

Modern CSS also introduces functional color manipulation, allowing developers to dynamically adjust colors or mix them.

| Function | Example | Description |
|---|---|---|
| currentColor | border-color: currentColor; | Inherits the element's `color` value. Useful for consistent designs. |
| color-mix() | color: color-mix(in srgb, red 50%, blue 50%); | Mixes two colors to create a new one (browser support is limited). |
| var() | color: var(--main-color); | Uses CSS custom properties (variables) to apply colors dynamically. |

**Practice Lab Guide**

**Objective:** Practice using different color values, transparency, and color functions to style a web page.

**Step 1: Set up HTML**

Create a simple HTML page with three boxes inside a container.

<!DOCTYPE html>

<html lang="en">

<head>

   <title>CSS Color Management Lab</title>

   <link rel="stylesheet" href="styles.css">

</head>

```
<body>
  <div class="container">
    <div class="box box1">Named Color</div>
    <div class="box box2">RGBA Color</div>
    <div class="box box3">HSL with Transparency</div>
  </div>
</body>
</html>
```

**Step 2: Apply CSS (styles.css)**

```
.container {
  display: flex;
  gap: 20px;
}

.box {
  width: 150px;
  height: 150px;
  display: flex;
  align-items: center;
  justify-content: center;
  color: white;
  font-weight: bold;
}
.box1 {
  background-color: tomato; /* Named color */
}

.box2 {
```

```
    background-color: rgba(0, 128, 255, 0.6); /* Semi-transparent blue */
}
.box3 {
    background-color: hsla(120, 100%, 40%, 0.7); /* Transparent green */
}
```

### Step 3: Try Modern Color Function (Optional, for supported browsers)

Add a new box that uses color-mix() (ensure browser support).

```
.box4 {
    background-color: color-mix(in srgb, orange 50%, purple 50%);
}
```

### Learning Checkpoints

- Can you correctly apply named colors, hex, RGB, and HSL?
- Do you understand the difference between rgb() and rgba()?
- How does hsla() adjust transparency?
- Can you mix colors using color-mix()?

### Additional Challenge (Optional)

- Set a global variable --theme-color in your CSS.
- Use var() to apply --theme-color to different elements.

```
:root {
    --theme-color: steelblue;
}
h1 {
    color: var(--theme-color);
}
```

## B. Working with Gradients

Applying Linear and Radial Gradients for Background and Element Styling

### Explanation

In CSS, gradients are smooth transitions between two or more colors. They allow developers to create visually appealing backgrounds and design elements without needing image files. CSS supports two primary types of gradients:

**Linear gradients:** Colors transition along a straight line (horizontal, vertical, or at any angle).
**Radial gradients:** Colors radiate outward from a central point (circular or elliptical).
*Gradients are defined using the background or background-image property, and they offer flexibility for custom color blending and placement.*

### Linear Gradients
#### Definition
A linear gradient creates a smooth color transition along a defined axis (horizontal, vertical, diagonal, etc.).

### Syntax
background: linear-gradient(direction, color1, color2, ...);

### Example
background: linear-gradient(to right, blue, green);

*This creates a gradient that flows from blue (left) to green (right).*

**Direction Options for Linear Gradients**

| Direction Keyword | Effect |
|---|---|
| to top | Bottom to top |
| to bottom | Top to bottom (default) |
| to left | Right to left |
| to right | Left to right |
| Angle (e.g., 45deg ) | Controls the exact angle of color flow |

## Example with Angle

background: linear-gradient(45deg, red, yellow);

## Multi-Stop Gradients

You can add more than two colors, and even define how much space each color takes using color stops.

## Example:

background: linear-gradient(to bottom, red 10%, yellow 30%, green 90%);

## Radial Gradients

### Definition

A radial gradient spreads outward from a center point, creating circular or elliptical color transitions.

## Syntax

background: radial-gradient(shape size at position, color1, color2, ...);

## Example

background: radial-gradient(circle, red, yellow, green);

Miquill Nyle

*This creates a circular gradient starting with red at the center, transitioning to yellow, and ending with green.*

**Controlling Shape and Size**

| Option | Description |
| --- | --- |
| circle | Forces the gradient to be circular |
| ellipse | Default, stretches to fit element shape |
| closest-side | Reaches the nearest side |
| farthest-corner | Reaches the farthest corner (default) |

**Example with Positioning:**
background: radial-gradient(circle at top left, blue, white);

*This places the center of the gradient in the top-left corner.*

**Combining Gradients with Other Backgrounds**
CSS allows stacking multiple backgrounds, including gradients and images, for complex designs.

**Example:**
background: linear-gradient(to right, rgba(0,0,0,0.5), rgba(0,0,0,0)), url('image.jpg');

**Practice Lab Guide**
**Objective:** Practice applying linear and radial gradients to create visually appealing backgrounds and design elements.

10

**Step 1: Set Up HTML**

Create a simple page with several elements to style.

```
<!DOCTYPE html>
<html lang="en">
<head>
  <title>CSS Gradients Lab</title>
  <link rel="stylesheet" href="styles.css">
</head>
<body>
  <h1>CSS Gradient Practice</h1>
  <div class="linear-box">Linear Gradient</div>
  <div class="radial-box">Radial Gradient</div>
</body>
</html>
```

**Step 2: Apply CSS (styles.css)**

```
body {
  font-family: Arial, sans-serif;
  text-align: center;
  padding: 50px;
}

.linear-box {
  width: 300px;
  height: 150px;
  margin: 20px auto;
  background: linear-gradient(to right, skyblue, pink);
  display: flex;
  align-items: center;
```

```
    justify-content: center;
    color: white;
    font-weight: bold;
}

.radial-box {
    width: 300px;
    height: 150px;
    margin: 20px auto;
    background: radial-gradient(circle at center, orange, white);
    display: flex;
    align-items: center;
    justify-content: center;
    font-weight: bold;
}
```

**Step 3: Explore Variations**
- Change the direction of the linear gradient.
- Add more colors to the gradient.
- Change the shape and position of the radial gradient.
- Try combining gradients with background images.

**Learning Checkpoints**
- Can you apply linear gradients with different directions?
- Can you create a radial gradient that fits the shape of an element?
- Can you use color stops to create multi-step gradients?
- Can you combine gradients and images into a single background?

**Additional Challenge**

Create a button styled with a gradient background and a hover effect that changes the gradient's direction.

```
.button {
    padding: 10px 20px;
    border: none;
    cursor: pointer;
    background: linear-gradient(to right, darkblue, lightblue);
    color: white;
    font-weight: bold;
    transition: background 0.5s;
}

.button:hover {
    background: linear-gradient(to bottom, darkblue, lightblue);
}
```

Miquill Nyle

# C. Using Box Shadows

Adding Depth and Emphasis with Customizable Box Shadows

## Explanation

In web design, shadows are a useful tool to create visual emphasis and the illusion of depth. CSS provides the box-shadow property, which allows developers to apply shadows to almost any element, enhancing its appearance and making it stand out from the background.

The box-shadow property offers full control over the size, position, blur, spread, and color of the shadow, allowing for both subtle and dramatic visual effects.

## Syntax of box-shadow

box-shadow: offset-x offset-y blur-radius spread-radius color;

| Value | Description |
|---|---|
| offset-x | Horizontal position (positive moves right, negative moves left) |
| offset-y | Vertical position (positive moves down, negative moves up) |
| blur-radius | Amount of blur (higher values make softer edges) |
| spread-radius | Expands or contracts the shadow size |
| color | Shadow color (supports named colors, hex, rgb, rgba) |

## Example
### Simple Shadow

box-shadow: 5px 5px 10px rgba(0, 0, 0, 0.5);

## This adds a shadow that:

- Moves 5px right and 5px down
- Has a 10px blur (soft edges)

14

- Uses a semi-transparent black color

**Inset Shadow**

CSS also supports inset shadows, which appear inside the element rather than outside.

**Syntax:** box-shadow: inset 3px 3px 5px rgba(0, 0, 0, 0.5);

*This creates a subtle inner shadow, often used to make elements like input fields appear recessed.*

**Multiple Shadows**

You can layer multiple shadows by separating them with commas.

**Syntax:** box-shadow: 3px 3px 5px rgba(0,0,0,0.5), -3px -3px 5px rgba(255,255,255,0.7);

*This technique is popular in neumorphism design.*

**Common Use Cases**

| Use Case | Example |
|---|---|
| Elevating Cards | Adding shadow to content cards to make them pop off the page |
| Button Emphasis | Applying a shadow to make buttons more noticeable |
| Hover Effects | Increasing shadow size when users hover over an element |

**Example:**

```
button:hover {
    box-shadow: 0 8px 16px rgba(0,0,0,0.3);
}
```

**Practice Lab Guide**

**Objective:** Learn how to apply box shadows for different visual effects on web page elements.

**Step 1: Set Up HTML**

```
<!DOCTYPE html>
<html lang="en">
<head>
    <title>Box Shadow Practice</title>
    <link rel="stylesheet" href="styles.css">
</head>
<body>
    <h1>Box Shadow Practice Lab</h1>
    <div class="box basic-shadow">Basic Shadow</div>
    <div class="box inset-shadow">Inset Shadow</div>
    <div class="box hover-shadow">Hover to See Shadow</div>
</body>
</html>
```

Step 2: Apply CSS (styles.css)

```
body {
    font-family: Arial, sans-serif;
    text-align: center;
    margin: 50px;
}

.box {
    width: 200px;
    height: 100px;
    margin: 20px auto;
    display: flex;
```

```
    align-items: center;
    justify-content: center;
    font-weight: bold;
    background-color: white;
    border: 1px solid #ccc;
}
/* Basic Shadow */
.basic-shadow {
    box-shadow: 5px 5px 15px rgba(0, 0, 0, 0.3);
}


/* Inset Shadow */
.inset-shadow {
    box-shadow: inset 5px 5px 15px rgba(0, 0, 0, 0.3);
}
/* Hover Shadow */
.hover-shadow {
    transition: box-shadow 0.3s ease;
}
.hover-shadow:hover {
    box-shadow: 0 8px 16px rgba(0, 0, 0, 0.5);
}
```

### Step 3: Experiment with Customization
- Change the color of the shadow to match the theme.
- Add multiple shadows (one dark, one light).
- Increase or decrease the blur-radius to control sharpness.
- Adjust the spread-radius to make shadows larger.

**Learning Checkpoints**

- Can you apply a basic shadow to an element?
- Can you apply an inset shadow?
- Can you create a hover effect that changes the shadow?
- Can you use multiple shadows for complex visual effects?

**Additional Challenge**

Create a call-to-action button with:

- A bright colored background
- A hover shadow that grows larger to catch attention
- An inset shadow to make the button look pressed when clicked

```
button {
    background-color: #007bff;
    color: white;
    border: none;
    padding: 10px 20px;
    cursor: pointer;
    box-shadow: 0 4px 10px rgba(0,0,0,0.3);
    transition: box-shadow 0.3s ease;
}
button:hover {
    box-shadow: 0 8px 20px rgba(0,0,0,0.5);
}

button:active {
    box-shadow: inset 2px 2px 5px rgba(0,0,0,0.5);
}
```

## D. Text Styling Essentials

Controlling Typography, Spacing, and Visual Appearance of Text

**Explanation**

Text styling is a fundamental aspect of web design. In CSS, developers use various properties to control the typography, spacing, alignment, and appearance of text. These properties ensure that text content is readable, visually appealing, and aligned with the overall design of the page.

**CSS offers a wide range of text styling properties, covering:**

- Font selection and size
- Text alignment and decoration
- Line height and letter spacing
- Text color and case transformation

**Key Text Styling Properties**

| Property | Purpose | Example |
| --- | --- | --- |
| font-family | Sets the typeface (font) | font-family: Arial, sans-serif; |
| font-size | Controls text size | font-size: 16px; |
| font-weight | Defines thickness of text | font-weight: bold; |
| font-style | Makes text italic | font-style: italic; |
| line-height | Sets spacing between lines | line-height: 1.5; |
| letter-spacing | Adjusts space between letters | letter-spacing: 2px; |
| word-spacing | Adjusts space between words | word-spacing: 5px; |
| text-align | Aligns text (left, center, right) | text-align: center; |
| text-decoration | Adds underline, overline, etc. | text-decoration: underline; |
| text-transform | Changes case (uppercase, lowercase) | text-transform: uppercase; |
| color | Sets text color | color: #333; |

**Examples**

**Example 1: Basic Heading Styling**

```
h1 {
    font-family: 'Georgia', serif;
    font-size: 36px;
    font-weight: bold;
    text-align: center;
    color: darkblue;
}
```

**Example 2: Paragraph Text**

```
p {
    font-family: Arial, sans-serif;
    font-size: 16px;
    line-height: 1.5;
    color: #555;
    text-align: justify;
}
```

**Example 3: Adding Letter Spacing and Transform**

```
h2 {
    text-transform: uppercase;
    letter-spacing: 3px;
    color: teal;
}
```

**Combining Text Styles**

You can combine multiple text properties to create visual hierarchy — such as using large, bold fonts for headings and smaller, lighter fonts for body text.

```css
h1 {
    font-family: 'Verdana', sans-serif;
    font-size: 32px;
    font-weight: bold;
    color: navy;
    text-align: center;
    text-transform: uppercase;
    letter-spacing: 2px;
}

p {
    font-family: 'Arial', sans-serif;
    font-size: 14px;
    line-height: 1.6;
    color: #444;
    text-align: justify;
}
```

**Practice Lab Guide**

**Objective:** Practice applying typography and text styling properties to different text elements (headings, paragraphs, links) on a web page.

**Step 1: Set Up HTML**

```html
<!DOCTYPE html>
<html lang="en">
<head>
    <title>Text Styling Practice</title>
    <link rel="stylesheet" href="styles.css">
```

```
</head>
<body>
   <h1>Main Heading</h1>
   <h2>Subheading Example</h2>
   <p>This is a paragraph demonstrating basic text styling using CSS.</p>
   <p class="special">This is a special paragraph with custom spacing and font
weight.</p>
   <a href="#">This is a link.</a>
</body>
</html>
```

**Step 2: Apply CSS (styles.css)**

```
/* General body text settings */
body {
   font-family: Arial, sans-serif;
   margin: 40px;
   line-height: 1.5;
   color: #333;
}

/* Headings */
h1 {
   font-family: 'Georgia', serif;
   font-size: 36px;
   font-weight: bold;
   text-align: center;
   text-transform: uppercase;
   letter-spacing: 2px;
   color: darkblue;
```

```
    }

h2 {
    font-size: 24px;
    color: teal;
    text-align: left;
}

/* Paragraphs */
p {
    font-size: 16px;
    text-align: justify;
    margin-bottom: 20px;
}

/* Special class for emphasis */
.special {
    font-weight: bold;
    letter-spacing: 2px;
    color: darkgreen;
}
/* Links */
a {
    text-decoration: none;
    color: royalblue;
}
a:hover {
    text-decoration: underline;
}
```

### Step 3: Practice and Explore

- Try changing the font-family for headings and paragraphs.
- Adjust font-size and line-height to improve readability.
- Add spacing between letters or words to create unique styles.
- Test different text-align options (left, center, right).
- Add hover effects to links for better user feedback.

### Learning Checkpoints

- Can you apply font-family, size, and weight correctly?
- Can you align text using text-align?
- Can you add spacing between letters and lines?
- Can you customize text color and case transformation?

### Additional Challenge

Create a card component with a title, description text, and a button, each styled differently to create visual contrast and hierarchy.

```
<div class="card">
    <h3 class="card-title">Welcome to Our Website</h3>
    <p class="card-text">We offer a variety of web development tutorials to help
you improve your skills.</p>
    <a href="#" class="card-button">Learn More</a>
</div>
.card {
  width: 300px;
  padding: 20px;
  border: 1px solid #ccc;
  box-shadow: 0 4px 8px rgba(0,0,0,0.1);
```

```
    font-family: Arial, sans-serif;
    background-color: #f9f9f9;
}
.card-title {
    font-size: 24px;
    font-weight: bold;
    margin-bottom: 10px;
}
.card-text {
    font-size: 14px;
    color: #555;
    margin-bottom: 15px;
}
.card-button {
    display: inline-block;
    padding: 8px 12px;
    background-color: royalblue;
    color: white;
    text-decoration: none;
    text-transform: uppercase;
    letter-spacing: 1px;
    font-weight: bold;
    transition: background-color 0.3s;
}
.card-button:hover {
    background-color: darkblue;
}
```

Miquill Nyle

## E. Applying Text Shadows

Enhancing Text Readability and Design with Shadow Effects

**Explanation**
Text shadows are a visual styling technique in CSS that allows developers to add a shadow effect to text content. This feature can be used to:

- Improve readability when text overlaps a complex background (such as images).
- Create decorative or stylistic effects, such as glowing text or embossed/engraved looks.
- Enhance contrast, making the text stand out more clearly from its surroundings.

*In CSS, this is controlled by the text-shadow property. This property allows you to set the horizontal offset, vertical offset, blur radius, and color of the shadow.*

**Syntax and Explanation**
text-shadow: horizontal-offset vertical-offset blur-radius color;

- Horizontal offset: Moves the shadow left or right. Positive values move it right; negative values move it left.
- Vertical offset: Moves the shadow up or down. Positive values move it down; negative values move it up.
- Blur radius: Determines how soft or sharp the shadow edges are. A higher value creates a softer (more blurred) shadow.
- Color: Specifies the shadow color, using named colors, hex codes, RGB, or HSL values.

**Example**
**Basic Text Shadow**
```
h1 {
  text-shadow: 2px 2px 5px rgba(0, 0, 0, 0.5);
}
```

*This example applies:*

- 2 pixels of horizontal offset (moves right)
- 2 pixels of vertical offset (moves down)
- 5 pixels of blur radius (soft shadow edges)
- Semi-transparent black shadow (rgba)

26

**Example with Glow Effect**

```
h2 {
   color: white;
   text-shadow: 0 0 8px royalblue;
}
```

- Horizontal and vertical offsets are both zero (shadow is directly behind the text).
- Blur radius is 8 pixels.
- Shadow color is royal blue, creating a glowing effect.

**Multiple Shadows**

CSS allows combining multiple shadows on the same text by separating each shadow with a comma.

```
p {
   text-shadow: 2px 2px 3px #555, -2px -2px 3px #ddd;
}
```

*This creates a double shadow effect:*

- A dark shadow offset to the bottom-right.
- A light shadow offset to the top-left.

**Practice Lab Guide**

**Objective :** Practice adding text shadows to headings, paragraphs, and links to enhance their appearance and readability.

**Step 1: Set Up HTML**

```
<!DOCTYPE html>
<html lang="en">
<head>
   <title>Text Shadow Practice</title>
   <link rel="stylesheet" href="styles.css">
</head>
<body>
   <h1>Welcome to CSS Text Shadows</h1>
   <h2>Enhance Text Visibility</h2>
   <p class="shadow-text">This paragraph demonstrates a subtle text shadow.</p>
   <p class="glow-text">This text glows using text-shadow.</p>
</body>
</html>
```

**Step 2: Apply CSS (styles.css)**

```css
/* General page settings */
body {
    font-family: Arial, sans-serif;
    background-color: #f0f0f0;
    padding: 40px;
    text-align: center;
}
/* Header with subtle shadow */
h1 {
    font-size: 36px;
    color: navy;
    text-shadow: 2px 2px 4px rgba(0,0,0,0.3);
}
/* Subheading with an embossed effect */
h2 {
    font-size: 28px;
    color: darkslategray;
    text-shadow: 1px 1px 0 #fff, -1px -1px 0 #000;
}

/* Paragraph with subtle shadow */
.shadow-text {
    font-size: 18px;
    color: #333;
    text-shadow: 1px 1px 3px rgba(0,0,0,0.2);
}
/* Paragraph with glowing effect */
.glow-text {
    font-size: 18px;
    color: white;
    background-color: #222;
    padding: 10px;
    text-shadow: 0 0 10px cyan;
}
```

**Step 3: Experiment**

- Try changing horizontal and vertical offsets to shift the shadow in different directions.
- Increase or decrease the blur radius to sharpen or soften the shadow.

- Apply different colors to match your website's color scheme.
- Try using multiple shadows to create embossed or 3D effects.

### Learning Checkpoints

- Can you apply a basic text shadow?
- Can you create a glowing text effect?
- Can you combine multiple shadows for creative effects?
- Can you apply shadows to different elements like headings, paragraphs, and buttons?

### Additional Challenge

Create a banner section with a heading and subtitle, both using text shadows to improve readability over a background image.

### Example HTML

```
<div class="banner">
   <h1>CSS Masterclass</h1>
    <p>Learn advanced styling techniques</p>
</div>
```

### Example CSS

```
.banner {
   height: 300px;
   background-image: url('background.jpg');
   background-size: cover;
   background-position: center;
   display: flex;
   flex-direction: column;
   justify-content: center;
   align-items: center;
   color: white;
   text-align: center;
}
.banner h1 {
   font-size: 48px;
   text-shadow: 3px 3px 6px rgba(0, 0, 0, 0.8);
}
.banner p {
   font-size: 18px;
   text-shadow: 2px 2px 4px rgba(0, 0, 0, 0.5);
}
```

### F. Rounded Corners and Shape Control

Creating Soft Edges and Custom Element Shapes with border-radius

**Explanation**

In CSS, the border-radius property is used to create rounded corners on elements. By default, HTML elements such as divs, images, and buttons have sharp 90-degree corners. With border-radius, developers can soften these edges or even transform elements into circular or elliptical shapes. This improves visual aesthetics and creates more modern, user-friendly designs.

The border-radius property is flexible — it allows setting uniform rounding for all corners or custom rounding for individual corners.

**Syntax**
```
element {
  border-radius: value;
}
```
- value: Can be specified in pixels (px), percentages (%), or em units.
- Higher values create more rounded corners.
- Percentage values are useful for creating circles when applied to square elements.

**Example: Basic Rounded Corners**
```
.box {
  width: 200px;
  height: 200px;
  background-color: lightblue;
  border-radius: 20px;
}
```

This makes the corners smoothly rounded with a 20-pixel radius.

**Example:** Creating a Circle
To create a perfect circle, the element must be square (equal width and height), and the border-radius must be set to 50%:

```
.circle {
  width: 100px;
  height: 100px;
```

```
    background-color: coral;
    border-radius: 50%;
}
```

**Example: Custom Rounding for Each Corner**
You can also round each corner individually using:
```
.element {
    border-top-left-radius: 10px;
    border-top-right-radius: 20px;
    border-bottom-right-radius: 30px;
    border-bottom-left-radius: 40px;
}
```

**Or shorthand:**
```
.element {
    border-radius: 10px 20px 30px 40px; /* Top-left, top-right, bottom-right,
bottom-left */
}
```

**Special Shape Effects**
You can combine border-radius with background gradients or box shadows to create stylish buttons, containers, or even speech bubbles.

Example - Speech Bubble:
```
.speech-bubble {
    background-color: lightgray;
    padding: 20px;
    width: 300px;
    border-radius: 15px;
    position: relative;
}
```

```
.speech-bubble::after {
    content: '';
    position: absolute;
    bottom: -10px;
    left: 30px;
    width: 0;
    height: 0;
    border: 10px solid transparent;
    border-top-color: lightgray;
}
```

**Practice Lab Guide**
**Objective:** Use border-radius to create rounded boxes, circles, and creative shapes for common elements like buttons, containers, and profile pictures.

**Step 1: Set Up HTML**

```
<!DOCTYPE html>
<html lang="en">
<head>
    <title>Border Radius Practice</title>
    <link rel="stylesheet" href="styles.css">
</head>
<body>
    <div class="box">Rounded Box</div>
    <div class="circle">Circle</div>
    <div class="custom-shape">Custom Shape</div>
</body>
</html>
```

**Step 2: Apply CSS (styles.css)**

```
/* Rounded box */
.box {
    width: 200px;
    height: 100px;
    background-color: skyblue;
    border-radius: 15px;
    text-align: center;
    line-height: 100px;
    margin-bottom: 20px;
}

/* Circular shape */
.circle {
    width: 100px;
    height: 100px;
    background-color: tomato;
    border-radius: 50%;
    display: flex;
    align-items: center;
    justify-content: center;
}

/* Custom shape with varied corners */
.custom-shape {
```

```
  width: 200px;
  height: 100px;
  background-color: palegreen;
  border-radius: 20px 0 50px 0;
  text-align: center;
  line-height: 100px;
}
```

### Step 3: Experiment

- Adjust the border-radius to make sharper or softer corners.
- Try combining border-radius with background gradients for stylish effects.
- Create custom shapes like speech bubbles, pill-shaped buttons, or badges.

### Learning Checkpoints

- Can you apply simple rounded corners?
- Can you create a circular element?
- Can you apply different rounding to each corner?
- Can you combine border-radius with other styles like shadows, gradients, or borders?

### Additional Challenge
Create a profile card that uses rounded corners for both the card and a profile picture inside it.

### Example HTML
```
<div class="profile-card">
  <img src="profile.jpg" alt="Profile Picture" class="profile-pic">
  <p class="username">Jane Doe</p>
</div>
```

### Example CSS
```
.profile-card {
  width: 250px;
  padding: 20px;
  background-color: white;
  border: 1px solid #ddd;
  border-radius: 15px;
  text-align: center;
  box-shadow: 0 0 10px rgba(0,0,0,0.1);
```

```
}
.profile-pic {
   width: 100px;
   height: 100px;
   border-radius: 50%;
   object-fit: cover;
   margin-bottom: 10px;
}
.username {
   font-size: 18px;
   color: #333;
}
```

## G. Border Images

Styling Element Borders Using Images for Decorative Effects

### Explanation

In CSS, borders are usually defined using solid lines, dashed lines, or similar styles. However, CSS also provides a more decorative option called border-image, which allows developers to use images as the border around an element.

With border-image, you can take a small image (such as a decorative pattern or artistic frame) and apply it to all four sides of an element's border. This is particularly useful for creating custom frames, textured borders, or creative visual effects.

### Syntax

```
element {
    border-image-source: url('border.png');
    border-image-slice: 30;
    border-image-width: 10px;
    border-image-outset: 5px;
    border-image-repeat: round;
}
```

### Explanation of Properties

| Property | Description |
| --- | --- |
| border-image-source | Specifies the image file to use as the border. |
| border-image-slice | Divides the image into 9 parts (corners, edges, center). |
| border-image-width | Sets the width of the border area. |
| border-image-outset | Defines how far the border extends outside the element. |
| border-image-repeat | Controls how the image repeats (options: stretch , repeat , round , space ). |

### Concept: The 9-Slice Scaling Model

The image is divided into 9 areas:

- 4 corners
- 4 edges (top, bottom, left, right)
- 1 center

Corners remain intact, edges can be stretched or repeated, and the center can either be shown or hidden.

**Example 1: Simple Decorative Border**

```
.box {
    width: 300px;
    height: 150px;
    border-width: 20px;
    border-image-source: url('fancy-border.png');
    border-image-slice: 30;
    border-image-repeat: stretch;
}
```

**Explanation**
- Image fancy-border.png is applied as the border.
- The image is sliced 30 pixels in from each edge.
- The sliced image is stretched to fit the border space.

**Example 2: Repeating Pattern Border**

```
.frame {
    width: 300px;
    height: 150px;
    border-width: 15px;
    border-image-source: url('pattern.png');
    border-image-slice: 20;
    border-image-repeat: repeat;
}
```

**Explanation**
- A pattern image is used.
- Each edge of the border is filled by repeating the sliced section.
- This works well for tiled designs such as floral borders or geometric patterns.

**Example 3: Outset Border**

```
.card {
    border: 10px solid transparent;
    border-image-source: url('artistic-frame.png');
    border-image-slice: 40;
    border-image-outset: 10px;
}
```

**Explanation**
The image border extends 10px outside the element's box, which can create a more prominent frame effect.

**Practice Lab Guide**
**Objective:** Learn to apply border images to elements, adjusting slicing, repeating, and positioning to create custom decorative effects.

**Step 1: Prepare the HTML**
```
<!DOCTYPE html>
<html lang="en">
<head>
   <title>Border Image Practice</title>
   <link rel="stylesheet" href="styles.css">
</head>
<body>
   <div class="decorative-box">Decorative Box</div>
   <div class="pattern-frame">Pattern Frame</div>
</body>
</html>
```

**Step 2: Create the CSS (styles.css)**
```
/* Decorative border using image */
.decorative-box {
   width: 300px;
   height: 150px;
   border-width: 20px;
   border-image-source: url('fancy-border.png');
   border-image-slice: 30;
   border-image-repeat: stretch;
   text-align: center;
   line-height: 150px;
   font-size: 18px;
}
/* Pattern border using repeating image */
.pattern-frame {
   width: 300px;
   height: 150px;
   border-width: 15px;
   border-image-source: url('pattern.png');
   border-image-slice: 20;
   border-image-repeat: repeat;
```

```
    text-align: center;
    line-height: 150px;
    font-size: 18px;
}
```

**Step 3: Experiment**

- Try different border images (floral, geometric, and hand-drawn).
- Change the border-image-slice to control how much of the image is used.
- Explore different repeats (stretch, round, repeat) to see how the image behaves.
- Try adjusting border-image-outset to extend the border outside the element.

**Learning Checkpoints**

- Can you apply an image-based border to a box?
- Can you create repeating patterned borders?
- Can you control how the image is sliced and stretched?
- Can you adjust the position and width of the image border?

**Additional Challenge**

Create a photo frame effect, where an image is placed inside a decorative border created with border-image.

**Example HTML**
```html
<div class="photo-frame">
   <img src="photo.jpg" alt="Sample Photo">
</div>
```

**Example CSS**
```css
.photo-frame {
   display: inline-block;
   border: 20px solid transparent;
   border-image-source: url('photo-frame.png');
   border-image-slice: 25;
   border-image-repeat: stretch;
}
.photo-frame img {
   display: block;
   width: 100%;       }
```

# H. Multi-Background Techniques

**Explanation**

In CSS, background properties allow developers to add visual styling to elements using colors, images, or gradients. Modern CSS supports the use of multiple backgrounds applied to a single element. This technique is known as multi-background layering.

With multi-background techniques, you can stack several background layers on top of each other within a single element's background area. Each layer can be:

- A solid color
- A background image
- A linear or radial gradient

These backgrounds layer from top to bottom — the first background listed is the top layer, and each successive background sits behind it.

**Syntax**
```
element {
   background: background1, background2, background3;
}
```

**Explanation**
Each background layer can use different types of backgrounds, such as:

| Background Type | Example |
|---|---|
| Solid color | background-color: lightblue; |
| Image | background-image: url('pattern.png'); |
| Gradient | background-image: linear-gradient(to right, red, blue); |

*When combining multiple backgrounds, they are separated by commas.*

**Example: Combining Image and Color**
```
.box {
   width: 400px;
   height: 300px;
   background:
      url('pattern.png') repeat,
      linear-gradient(to bottom, rgba(255,255,255,0.5), rgba(0,0,0,0.5)),
```

```
    lightblue;
}
```

### Explanation
- Top layer: Repeating pattern image.
- Middle layer: Semi-transparent gradient overlay.
- Bottom layer: Solid light blue background.

### Example: Adding Multiple Background Images
```
.banner {
    width: 500px;
    height: 200px;
    background:
        url('stars.png') no-repeat center,
        url('clouds.png') repeat-x,
        skyblue;
}
```

### Explanation
- Top layer: Stars image, centered.
- Middle layer: Clouds image, tiled horizontally.
- Bottom layer: Solid sky blue background.

### Background Positioning
Each background can have its own position, size, and repeat settings.

```
background-image: url('pattern.png'), url('texture.png');
background-repeat: repeat, no-repeat;
background-position: top left, center;
background-size: auto, cover;
```

### Explanation
- First background (pattern) repeats fully.
- Second background (texture) is centered and covers the element.

### Why Use Multi-Backgrounds?
Multi-background techniques allow developers to: ✅ Create layered visual effects

- Add decorative images while maintaining a solid or gradient backdrop

- Apply overlays like gradients to images for better readability (e.g., banner text)
- Build complex visual styles with cleaner, less HTML markup

**Practice Lab Guide**
**Objective:** Learn how to apply multiple backgrounds to a single element and control their order, positioning, and appearance.

**Step 1: Create Basic HTML**

```
<!DOCTYPE html>
<html lang="en">
<head>
  <title>Multi-Background Practice</title>
  <link rel="stylesheet" href="styles.css">
</head>
<body>
  <div class="layered-box">Layered Background Example</div>
</body>
</html>
```

**Step 2: Apply CSS (styles.css)**

```
.layered-box {
  width: 500px;
  height: 300px;
  font-size: 20px;
  display: flex;
  align-items: center;
  justify-content: center;
  color: white;
  background:
    url('stars.png') no-repeat center,
    linear-gradient(to bottom, rgba(0, 0, 0, 0.5), transparent),
    skyblue;
  background-size: cover, cover, cover;
  text-shadow: 2px 2px 4px rgba(0,0,0,0.7);
}
```

**Step 3: Experiment**

- Swap out images and gradients.

- Change the order of the backgrounds to see how stacking changes the appearance.
- Use background-size to resize each layer independently.
- Try adding background-blend-mode to experiment with blending (optional advanced step).

**Learning Checkpoints**

- Can you layer an image over a gradient?
- Can you apply multiple images on the same element?
- Can you control repetition, size, and position for each background?
- Can you combine a solid color with a decorative image for subtle effects?

**Additional Challenge**
Create a website banner with a background that combines:

- A sky-blue gradient at the base.
- A cloud image repeating across the width.
- A brand logo centered in the banner.

**Example HTML**
```
<header class="hero-banner">
  <h1>Welcome to Our Site</h1>
</header>
```

**Example CSS**
```
.hero-banner {
  height: 200px;
  display: flex;
  align-items: center;
  justify-content: center;
  color: white;
  font-size: 30px;
  background:
    url('logo.png') no-repeat center,
    url('clouds.png') repeat-x,
    linear-gradient(to bottom, skyblue, lightblue);
  background-size: auto, contain, cover;
  text-shadow: 2px 2px 5px rgba(0, 0, 0, 0.5);
}
```

## I. Box Decoration Breaks

### What is "Box Decoration Breaks"?

When you style an element (like a paragraph, div, or section) using borders, padding, or backgrounds, those styles usually cover the entire element as a whole box. But, sometimes, when the content inside that element gets split across multiple lines or pages (in print styles), you might want to control what happens to those decorations — like, should the border restart at the top of the new page? Should the background color flow continuously across the break?

This is where box-decoration-break comes into play. This CSS property allows you to manage how box decorations behave when content splits into different boxes.

### Examples of Element Boundaries
- When text inside a <p> spans multiple columns in a newspaper-style layout (like using column-count in CSS).
- When content breaks across pages in a print stylesheet.
- When inline elements (like a link <a>) wrap onto a new line.

### The box-decoration-break Property
This property controls how decorations like:

- Borders
- Padding
- Backgrounds

behave when content breaks across boxes (like pages, columns, or lines).

### Syntax
box-decoration-break: slice | clone;

### Explanation of Values

| Value | Meaning |
|-------|---------|
| slice | Decorations (like background and border) **do not restart** at each break. They flow **continuously**. This is like treating the whole thing as **one single box**. |
| clone | Decorations **restart** at each break. Each piece (page, column, or line) gets a **complete decoration** applied to it separately. Each split part acts like its own box. |

### Example 1 — Using box-decoration-break
Imagine you have a long paragraph inside a multi-column layout.

```
<div class="multi-column-text">
 This is some long text that will flow across multiple columns.
</div>
```

```
.multi-column-text {
    column-count: 2;
    background: lightblue;
    border: 5px solid navy;
    padding: 10px;
    box-decoration-break: slice;
}
```

With slice, the background and border flow continuously across columns — as if the whole text block is one single box.

If you change it to clone:

```
box-decoration-break: clone;
```

Now, each column gets its own separate background, border, and padding — each piece is treated like a new individual box.

### Real-life Use Case Example
**Magazine Layout**

If you're designing a digital magazine with a 2-column format, you might want each column to have its own border and padding, making them look like individual boxes. In that case, you would use:
box-decoration-break: clone;

If you want the content to feel like one continuous flowing piece, you would use:
box-decoration-break: slice;

### Practice Lab Guide
**Objective:** Understand how box decorations behave across column breaks.

**Steps**

1. Create an HTML file with a long paragraph of text.
2. Apply column-count: 3 to a container div.
3. Add background color, padding, and border to that div.
4. Try box-decoration-break: slice and box-decoration-break: clone.
5. Observe how the styles change across columns.

**Sample Code to Try**

```
<!DOCTYPE html>
<html lang="en">
<head>
  <style>
    .column-box {
      column-count: 3;
      padding: 20px;
      border: 4px solid darkgreen;
      background-color: lightyellow;
      box-decoration-break: slice; /* Change to clone and see the difference */
    }
  </style>
</head>
<body>

<div class="column-box">
  Lorem ipsum dolor sit amet, consectetur adipiscing elit. Sed do eiusmod tempor
incididunt ut labore et dolore magna aliqua. Ut enim ad minim veniam, quis
nostrud exercitation ullamco laboris nisi ut aliquip ex ea commodo consequat.
</div>

</body>
</html>
```

**What to Observe**
- With slice, the border and background flow as if it's one continuous box.
- With clone, each column gets its own separate border and background.

**Summary Table**

| Use Case | Recommended Setting |
| --- | --- |
| One continuous flowing design (like a single article split across columns) | slice |
| Each section should feel independent (like separate article excerpts) | clone |

## J. <u>Caret and Selection Styling</u>

Customizing the appearance of the text cursor and selected text

**What is the Caret?**
The caret is the blinking text cursor you see when typing in an input field, text area, or editable content area. It shows the insertion point—where your next typed character will appear.

**Example:** When you click inside a text box, the little blinking line is the caret.

**What is Selection?**
Selection refers to the part of the text you highlight when you click and drag with your mouse (or use Shift + arrow keys). The default appearance of selected text is usually a blue background with white text (this varies by browser and operating system).

**Example:**
If you highlight this:
Example Text

The **highlighted area** is the **selection**.

**Customizing Caret and Selection Styling**
Modern CSS allows you to change how both the caret and selected text look to match your design or branding.

**CSS Properties for Caret & Selection**

| Type | Property/Selector | What it does |
|------|-------------------|--------------|
| Caret | caret-color | Changes the color of the blinking text cursor. |
| Selection | ::selection | Changes the background color and text color when text is highlighted (selected). |

**Examples of Caret and Selection Styling**
**Example 1 — Caret Color**

```
<input type="text" class="custom-caret">
```

```
.custom-caret {
```

```
    caret-color: red; /* Makes the blinking cursor red */
    font-size: 18px;
}
```

**What happens?**
The caret (blinking cursor) inside the input will appear red instead of the default black.

Example 2 — Custom Selection Styling
```
<p class="custom-selection">Highlight this text to see custom selection styling.</p>
```

```
.custom-selection::selection {
    background-color: gold; /* Background of selected text */
    color: black; /* Text color of selected text */
}
```

**Practice Lab Guide**
**Objective:** Learn how to style both caret and selected text.

**Steps**
1. Create an HTML file with an input box and a paragraph.
2. Add caret-color to the input box to change the blinking cursor.
3. Add ::selection to the paragraph to style the selected text.
4. Test by typing in the input and highlighting text in the paragraph.

**Sample Code for Practice**
```
<!DOCTYPE html>
<html lang="en">
<head>
  <style>
    input {
      caret-color: magenta;
      font-size: 18px;
      padding: 5px;
    }
    p::selection {
      background-color: lime;
      color: darkblue;
    }
  </style>
</head>
```

```
<body>

<h3>Try Custom Caret & Selection Styling</h3>

<label>Type something:</label>
<input type="text">

<p>Select this text to see selection styling in action.</p>

</body>
</html>
```

### What to Observe?

- When you type in the input box, the caret (cursor) will be magenta.
- When you highlight the paragraph text, the selection will have a lime background and dark blue text.

### Quick Summary Table

| Styling | Property/Selector | Example |
|---|---|---|
| Caret (Cursor) | caret-color | caret-color: red; |
| Selected Text | ::selection | p::selection { background-color: yellow; } |

### When to Use This?

| Scenario | What to Style |
|---|---|
| Brand Customization | Matching the caret and selection color to your brand's color scheme. |
| Theming/Dark Mode | Making selection colors work better in dark mode. |
| Accessibility | Improving visibility of selection for better readability. |

### Pro Tip

- caret-color works in input, textarea, and content-editable areas.
- ::selection works almost everywhere, but not on images or some non-text elements.

# K. <u>2D Transforms</u>

## What are 2D Transforms?

2D Transforms allow you to move, rotate, scale, or skew elements in a two-dimensional space — meaning along the X-axis (horizontal) and Y-axis (vertical).

This is part of CSS, and it helps to apply cool effects like:

- Rotating an image.
- Scaling a button to make it bigger when hovered.
- Moving a text box to the left or right.
- Skewing a shape to make it look slanted.

## Why Use 2D Transforms?

- To create dynamic, interactive designs.
- To apply creative animations.
- To improve visual appeal in user interfaces (buttons, images, text blocks, etc.).

## Types of 2D Transforms

| Transform Type | Description | Example |
|---|---|---|
| rotate() | Rotates the element by an angle (in degrees) | rotate(45deg) |
| scale() | Resizes the element (bigger or smaller) | scale(1.5) |
| translate() | Moves the element along X or Y axis | translate(50px, 20px) |
| skew() | Slants the element along X or Y axis | skew(20deg, 10deg) |

## Examples

### Example 1 — Rotate
Rotating an image 45 degrees:
img {
    transform: rotate(45deg);
}

### Example 2 — Scale
Making a button 1.5 times bigger:
button {

```
    transform: scale(1.5);
}
```

**Example 3 — Translate (Move)**
Moving a box 100px to the right and 50px down:
```
.box {
    transform: translate(100px, 50px);
}
```

**Example 4 — Skew**
Slanting a box:
```
.box {
    transform: skew(20deg, 10deg);
}
```

**You Can Combine Multiple Transforms**
```
.box {
    transform: rotate(30deg) translate(50px, 0) scale(1.2);
}
```

*This rotates the element, moves it 50px to the right, and makes it 1.2 times larger — all at once!*

**Practice Lab Guide**
**Objective:** Learn to apply and experiment with different 2D transform types.

**Setup**
Create an HTML file with some elements like a box, image, and button. Apply transforms to each.

**Sample HTML + CSS**
```
<!DOCTYPE html>
<html lang="en">
<head>
  <style>
    .box {
      width: 100px;
      height: 100px;
      background-color: lightcoral;
      margin: 20px;
```

```
        display: inline-block;
      }
      .rotate {
        transform: rotate(45deg);
      }
      .scale {
        transform: scale(1.5);
      }
      .translate {
        transform: translate(50px, 50px);
      }
      .skew {
        transform: skew(20deg, 10deg);
      }
  </style>
</head>
<body>

<h2>2D Transforms Practice</h2>

<div class="box rotate">Rotate</div>
<div class="box scale">Scale</div>
<div class="box translate">Translate</div>
<div class="box skew">Skew</div>

</body>
</html>
```

**What to Do**
- Try changing the values inside rotate(), scale(), translate(), and skew().
- Add :hover so the transformations only happen when you hover over the box.
- Combine multiple transforms like transform: rotate(30deg) scale(1.2).

**Quick Summary Table**

| Transform | Example | What it Does |
|---|---|---|
| Rotate | rotate(45deg) | Rotates element by 45 degrees |
| Scale | scale(2) | Doubles the size of the element |
| Translate | translate(50px, 100px) | Moves 50px right. 100px down |
| Skew | skew(20deg, 10deg) | Slants the element horizontally and vertically |

### Real-Life Examples

| Example | Explanation |
|---|---|
| Image Gallery | Rotate images slightly for a scrapbook effect |
| Buttons | Scale buttons bigger when hovered |
| Animations | Translate elements to slide into view |
| Text Effects | Skew text for creative typography |

### Pro Tip

Combine 2D Transforms with transitions for smooth animations:

```
.box {
    transition: transform 0.5s ease;
}
.box:hover {
    transform: scale(1.2) rotate(10deg);
}
```

## L. 3D Transforms

### What are 3D Transforms?

3D transforms allow you to move, rotate, and scale elements in three-dimensional space — adding the Z-axis to your usual X-axis (horizontal) and Y-axis (vertical).

In simple words:

2D Transforms work like flat paper (X and Y).
3D Transforms add depth (Z-axis), so you can push elements closer to the screen or farther away (like popping out of the screen).

### Why Use 3D Transforms?
- To create depth effects, like flipping cards or rotating cubes.
- To make elements feel more realistic by adding perspective.
- To build interactive UI components that respond to mouse movements in 3D.

### Key 3D Transform Properties

| Property | What It Does |
|---|---|
| transform | Applies rotation, scaling, or translation in 3D space. |
| perspective | Adds a sense of **depth**, simulating the way things look farther or closer. |
| transform-style | Controls how children behave in 3D space (flat or nested 3D). |

## Types of 3D Transforms

| Type | Description | Example |
|---|---|---|
| rotateX() | Rotates the element around the **horizontal axis** | rotateX(45deg) |
| rotateY() | Rotates the element around the **vertical axis** | rotateY(45deg) |
| rotateZ() | Rotates the element like turning a knob (Z is still like 2D rotation) | rotateZ(45deg) |
| translateZ() | Moves element **closer** (positive) or **farther** (negative) along Z-axis | translateZ(100px) |
| scaleZ() | Scales element along the Z-axis | scaleZ(2) |

### Understanding Perspective

- Perspective is like adding a "camera" view to the page.
- It controls how much depth effect you see.
- Smaller values = stronger perspective (more dramatic depth).
- Larger values = weaker perspective (flatter).

```
.container {
   perspective: 600px;
}
```

### Examples

### Example 1 — RotateX
Tilting a card back (like flipping it open):
```
.card {
   transform: rotateX(45deg);
}
```

### Example 2 — RotateY
Spinning a div left or right:
```
.card {
   transform: rotateY(60deg);
}
```

### Example 3 — Adding Perspective
To make 3D transforms look natural, you wrap the element in a container with perspective:
```
<div class="scene">
   <div class="box">3D Box</div>
</div>
```

```
.scene {
   perspective: 500px;
}
.box {
   transform: rotateY(45deg);
   width: 100px;
   height: 100px;
   background-color: lightcoral;
```

```
}
```

**Practice Lab Guide**
**Objective:** Create a 3D flipping card using perspective, rotateX, and rotateY.

**Steps**
1. Create a card with a front and back side.
2. Apply perspective to the card container.
3. Use rotateY to flip the card.
4. Add hover effect to trigger the flip.

**Sample Code for Practice**
```html
<!DOCTYPE html>
<html lang="en">
<head>
  <style>
    .scene {
      perspective: 600px;
      width: 200px;
      height: 300px;
    }
    .card {
      width: 100%;
      height: 100%;
      transform-style: preserve-3d;
      transition: transform 1s;
    }
    .scene:hover .card {
      transform: rotateY(180deg);
    }
    .card-side {
      position: absolute;
      width: 100%;
      height: 100%;
      backface-visibility: hidden;
      display: flex;
      align-items: center;
      justify-content: center;
      font-size: 24px;
      font-weight: bold;
    }
```

```
      .front {
        background-color: lightblue;
      }
      .back {
        background-color: lightcoral;
        transform: rotateY(180deg);
      }
  </style>
</head>
<body>

<h3>Hover over the card to flip it!</h3>
<div class="scene">
  <div class="card">
    <div class="card-side front">Front</div>
    <div class="card-side back">Back</div>
  </div>
</div>

</body>
</html>
```

**What to Observe**

- The container adds perspective.
- The card rotates when hovered.
- transform-style: preserve-3d ensures both sides exist in 3D space.
- backface-visibility: hidden hides the back until the flip.

**Quick Summary Table**

| 3D Transform | Example | What It Does |
| --- | --- | --- |
| RotateX | rotateX(45deg) | Tilts element back/forward |
| RotateY | rotateY(45deg) | Spins element left/right |
| RotateZ | rotateZ(45deg) | Rotates element flat (2D style) |
| TranslateZ | translateZ(100px) | Moves element closer/farther |
| Perspective | perspective: 500px | Adds depth effect |

**Real-Life Use Cases**

| Example | Use Case |
|---|---|
| Flipping Cards | For portfolios, product previews, game cards |
| 3D Buttons | Buttons that "pop out" when hovered |
| Cube Animation | Rotating cubes for galleries |
| Parallax Scrolling | Background moves sl ⤓ er than foreground |

**Pro Tip**

- Always apply perspective to a parent container, not the element itself.
- Use transform-style: preserve-3d if children also need to exist in 3D.
- Combine 3D transforms with transitions for smooth effects.

Miquill Nyle

# M. <u>Transitions</u>

### What are Transitions?

Transitions in CSS allow you to create smooth animations when elements change from one state to another.

Without transitions, changes like color changes, size adjustments, or position shifts happen instantly. With transitions, these changes become gradual over a period of time — adding a professional and polished look to your web pages.

### What Can You Animate with Transitions?

You can apply transitions to any animatable property, such as:

| Property | Example |
|---|---|
| color | Text color changes from black to red |
| background-color | Button background changes from gray to blue |
| transform | An element rotates, scales, or moves |
| opacity | Fading in/out effects |
| height/width | Expanding or shrinking elements |

### Syntax Breakdown
element {
    transition: property duration timing-function delay;
}

| Part | Meaning | Example |
|---|---|---|
| property | What you want to animate | background-color |
| duration | How long the animation lasts | 0.5s |
| timing-function | Speed curve (ease, linear, etc.) | ease-in-out |
| delay | Time to wait before animation starts | 0s |

### Example 1 — Color Change Transition
button {
    background-color: lightblue;
    transition: background-color 0.5s ease;
}

58

```
button:hover {
   background-color: navy;
}
```

**What happens?**
The button background smoothly changes from light blue to navy when hovered.

### Example 2 — Size Change Transition

```
.box {
   width: 100px;
   height: 100px;
   background-color: coral;
   transition: width 1s ease-in-out;
}
.box:hover {
   width: 200px;
}
```

**What happens?**
The box expands smoothly when hovered.

### Example 3 — Multiple Properties

You can transition more than one property at once:

```
.box {
   width: 100px;
   height: 100px;
   background-color: coral;
   transition: width 1s, background-color 0.5s;
}
.box:hover {
   width: 200px;
   background-color: lightgreen;
}
```

**What happens?**
The box expands and its color changes at the same time.

**Practice Lab Guide**
**Objective:** Learn how to use transitions to create smooth hover effects on a button, box, and text.

**Instructions**
1. Create an HTML file with a button, a box, and a paragraph.
2. Apply different transitions to each (color change, size change, text color change).
3. Use :hover to trigger the transition.
4. Experiment with different timing-functions like ease, linear, ease-in-out.

**Sample Code for Practice**
```
<!DOCTYPE html>
<html lang="en">
<head>
  <style>
    body {
      font-family: Arial, sans-serif;
    }

    .btn {
      background-color: skyblue;
      color: black;
      padding: 10px 20px;
      border: none;
      cursor: pointer;
      transition: background-color 0.5s ease, color 0.5s ease;
    }

    .btn:hover {
      background-color: navy;
      color: white;
    }

    .box {
      width: 100px;
      height: 100px;
      background-color: coral;
      transition: transform 0.5s ease;
    }

    .box:hover {
      transform: scale(1.5);
```

```
        }

     p {
        font-size: 16px;
        color: black;
        transition: color 0.5s linear;
     }

     p:hover {
        color: darkgreen;
     }
   </style>
</head>
<body>

<h3>CSS Transitions Practice</h3>

<button class="btn">Hover me</button>
<br><br>
<div class="box">Box</div>
<br>
<p>Hover over this text</p>

</body>
</html>
```

**What to Do**
Hover over each element and observe:

- The button's background and text color change smoothly.
- The box grows bigger.
- The text color changes smoothly.

**Quick Summary Table**

| Property | Meaning | Example |
|---|---|---|
| property | What you want to animate | background-color |
| duration | Length of animation | 0.5s |
| timing-function | Speed curve | ease-in-out |
| delay | When to start animation | 0s |

### Real-Life Examples of Transitions

| Example | Why Use It? |
| --- | --- |
| Navigation Menus | Smooth opening/closing effect |
| Buttons | Professional hover effects |
| Cards | Hover zoom or color change |
| Image Galleries | Smooth scaling or opacity change |

### Pro Tip
For super smooth and modern-looking transitions, try:
transition: all 0.3s ease;

*This applies a smooth transition to everything that can change.*

### Timing Function Cheat Sheet

| Timing Function | Effect |
| --- | --- |
| ease | Starts slow, speeds up, slows down |
| linear | Constant speed |
| ease-in | Starts slow |
| ease-out | Ends slow |
| ease-in-out | Starts and ends slow |

# N. <u>CSS Animations</u>

## What are CSS Animations?

CSS Animations allow you to create complex, multi-step animations directly in your CSS. Unlike simple transitions (which only animate between two states, like hover), animations can go through several stages using keyframes.

## Key Differences: Transitions vs Animations

| Feature | Transitions | Animations |
|---|---|---|
| Number of Steps | 2 (start & end) | Multiple (custom steps) |
| Control | Triggered by events like hover | Can start automatically & loop |
| Keyframes | Not used | Uses @keyframes to define steps |
| Repetition | Runs once (unless triggered again) | Can loop infinitely or set number of times |

## Anatomy of a CSS Animation
A CSS Animation has two main parts:

## 1. The @keyframes Rule (What Happens)
This defines the steps (keyframes) of the animation.

```
@keyframes slideIn {
    from {
        transform: translateX(-100%);
    }
    to {
        transform: translateX(0);
    }
}
```

## 2. The Animation Property (When & How)
This is applied to the element to control:

- Duration
- Timing function (speed curve)
- Delay
- Number of times it repeats
- Whether it plays forward, backward, or both

```
.box {
  animation: slideIn 1s ease-out;
}
```

### Example 1 — Simple Slide-in Animation

```
@keyframes slideIn {
  from {
    transform: translateX(-100%);
  }
  to {
    transform: translateX(0);
  }
}

.box {
  animation: slideIn 1s ease-out;
}
```

### Example 2 — Multi-Step Animation (Color & Rotation)

```
@keyframes spinAndColor {
  0% {
    transform: rotate(0deg);
    background-color: coral;
  }
  50% {
    transform: rotate(180deg);
    background-color: lightgreen;
  }
  100% {
    transform: rotate(360deg);
    background-color: lightblue;
  }
}

.box {
  animation: spinAndColor 2s ease-in-out infinite;
}
```

*This will:*

- Rotate the box a full 360 degrees.
- Change the color at different points.
- Repeat forever (infinite).

## Animation Shorthand

animation: name duration timing-function delay iteration-count direction;

| Property | What It Does | Example |
|---|---|---|
| name | Keyframes name | spinAndColor |
| duration | Total time | 2s |
| timing-function | Speed curve | ease-in-out |
| delay | Wait time before starting | 0s |
| iteration-count | How many times to repeat | infinite |
| direction | Forward, reverse, or alternate | alternate |

## Practice Lab Guide

**Objective:** Create a box that bounces, changes color, and spins using keyframes.

## Instructions

1. Set up a simple HTML page with a div element.
2. Use @keyframes to define multiple steps.
3. Apply the animation to the box.
4. Add properties like infinite or alternate to explore effects.

## Sample Practice Code

```
<!DOCTYPE html>
<html lang="en">
<head>
  <style>
    .box {
      width: 100px;
      height: 100px;
      background-color: coral;
      position: relative;
      animation: bounceSpin 3s ease-in-out infinite alternate;
    }

    @keyframes bounceSpin {
```

```
        0% {
            top: 0;
            transform: rotate(0deg);
            background-color: coral;
        }
        50% {
            top: 100px;
            transform: rotate(180deg);
            background-color: lightgreen;
        }
        100% {
            top: 0;
            transform: rotate(360deg);
            background-color: skyblue;
        }
    }
  </style>
</head>
<body>

<h3>CSS Animations Practice: Bouncing Box</h3>
<div class="box"></div>

</body>
</html>
```

**What Happens Here**
- The box bounces down and up.
- It also spins 360 degrees.
- The color changes at every stage.
- It repeats forever (infinite), going forward, then backward (thanks to alternate).

### Quick Summary Table

| Property | Example | What It Does |
|---|---|---|
| animation-name | bounceSpin | Links to the @keyframes name |
| animation-duration | 3s | Total time for one cycle |
| animation-timing-function | ease-in-out | Speed curve |
| animation-delay | 0s | Starts right away |
| animation-iteration-count | infinite | Loops forever |
| animation-direction | alternate | Plays forward then backward |

### Real-Life Use Cases for CSS Animations

| Example | Use Case |
|---|---|
| Loading Spinners | Spinning icons while waiting |
| Notification Popups | Slide-in/out alerts |
| Image Slideshows | Fading or sliding images |
| Buttons | Attention-grabbing wobbles or pulses |
| Progress Bars | Animating progress changes |

### Pro Tip: Combine Animations with Events

You can trigger animations on hover, click, or scroll to make them interactive.

```
.box {
    animation: none; /* default state */
}
.box:hover {
    animation: bounceSpin 2s ease;
}
```

### Advanced Tip: Multiple Animations at Once

You can apply more than one animation to the same element:

```
.box {
    animation: bounce 2s ease-in-out infinite, spin 1s linear infinite;
}
```

# O. <u>Multi-Column Layouts</u>

### What are Multi-Column Layouts?

A multi-column layout in CSS allows you to split text (or content) into multiple vertical columns, similar to the layout in newspapers or magazines. This is useful for displaying long text content in a way that's easier to read across wide screens.

### Why Use Multi-Column Layouts?

- They improve readability for long articles.
- They are responsive, adapting to different screen sizes.
- They are easy to create with just a few CSS properties.

### Core Properties of Multi-Column Layouts

| Property | What It Does | Example |
|---|---|---|
| column-count | Number of columns | column-count: 3; |
| column-width | Minimum width for each column (browser fits as many as possible) | column-width: 200px; |
| column-gap | Space between columns | column-gap: 20px; |
| column-rule | Line between columns (like a border) | column-rule: 1px solid black; |

### Example 1 — Simple 3-Column Layout
```
.article {
    column-count: 3;
    column-gap: 20px;
    column-rule: 1px solid lightgray;
}
```

*This divides the text into 3 columns, with 20px space between each column and a thin gray line between columns.*

### Example 2 — Flexible Column Width
```
.article {
    column-width: 250px;
    column-gap: 15px;
}
```

68

*This allows the browser to fit as many 250px columns as possible in the container width. If the screen is narrow, fewer columns appear.*

### Example 3 — Combining Both Approaches

```
.article {
    column-count: 3;
    column-width: 200px;
    column-gap: 25px;
    column-rule: 2px dashed darkgray;
}
```

*This sets a goal of 3 columns, but the column-width limits each column to at least 200px. The gap between columns is 25px and the columns are separated by a dashed line.*

### Quick Property Summary

| Property | Description | Example |
|---|---|---|
| column-count | Number of columns | `column-count: 2;` |
| column-width | Minimum width per column | `column-width: 200px;` |
| column-gap | Space between columns | `column-gap: 20px;` |
| column-rule | Line between columns | `column-rule: 1px solid black;` |

### Practice Lab Guide

**Objective:** Create an article layout with multiple columns that adapts to different screen sizes.

### Instructions

1. Create an HTML file with an article (<p> or <div> with lots of text).
2. Apply CSS to turn it into a 3-column layout.
3. Add a gap between columns and a rule (line) between them.
4. Try using both column-count and column-width to see how they behave.

### Sample Practice Code

```
<!DOCTYPE html>
<html lang="en">
<head>
  <style>
    body {
        font-family: Arial, sans-serif;
        padding: 20px;
    }
```

69

```
    .article {
        column-count: 3;
        column-gap: 20px;
        column-rule: 2px solid lightgray;
    }
    </style>
</head>
<body>

<h3>Multi-Column Layout Example</h3>
<div class="article">
    Lorem ipsum dolor sit amet, consectetur adipiscing elit. Quisque sodales lorem
et suscipit auctor.
    Nulla facilisi. Donec nec lacus eget sapien congue suscipit. In hac habitasse
platea dictumst.
    Curabitur quis libero nec ligula efficitur commodo. Vivamus ullamcorper nunc
eget purus mattis,
    id pharetra urna vestibulum. Ut imperdiet enim ac arcu facilisis, non pharetra
justo feugiat.
    Aliquam erat volutpat. Suspendisse potenti.
</div>

</body>
</html>
```

### What to Do
- Try resizing the browser to see how columns adjust.
- Experiment with column-width to let the browser decide the number of columns.
- Add more text to see how columns fill up.

### Real-Life Uses for Multi-Column Layouts

| Example | Use Case |
| --- | --- |
| News Websites | Articles formatted like newspapers |
| Blog Posts | Long-form content broken into columns |
| Product Descriptions | Technical specifications in side-by-side columns |
| Legal Documents | Terms and conditions pages |

**Pro Tip**
You can combine multi-column layouts with responsive design techniques (like media queries) to create layouts that switch between single-column on mobile and multi-column on desktop.

```
.article {
    column-width: 250px;
    column-gap: 20px;
}
@media (max-width: 600px) {
    .article {
        column-count: 1;
    }
}
```

**Summary Table — Multi-Column Cheat Sheet**

| Property | Purpose | Example |
|---|---|---|
| column-count | Number of columns | column-count: 3; |
| column-width | Minimum column width | column-width: 200px; |
| column-gap | Space between columns | column-gap: 15px; |
| column-rule | Line between columns | column-rule: 1px solid black; |

**Bonus: Span Across All Columns**
Sometimes you want a heading to span across all columns.
```
h1 {
    column-span: all;
}
```

## Book Synopsis

*Cascading Style Sheets Rock Star – Book 2: Techniques Every Web Developer Should Know* provides web developers with a practical guide to enhancing their CSS skills through essential styling techniques. This book focuses on topics that are critical for creating visually appealing, user-friendly, and modern web interfaces.

Covering areas such as **color management, gradients, shadows,** and **rounded corners**, the book offers techniques for adding polish and depth to web elements. Developers will also learn how to work with **border images**, apply **multi-background layers**, and manage **box decoration breaks**, allowing them to build more complex visual designs with confidence.

The book further explores **caret color** customization, **text selection styling**, and advanced **text and typography controls**, ensuring content remains both readable and aesthetically pleasing. Additionally, developers will gain hands-on knowledge of **2D and 3D transforms, transitions,** and **animations**, enabling them to introduce motion and interactivity into their designs.

To round out these essential techniques, the book covers **multi-column layouts,** providing developers with tools to efficiently structure text-heavy content for improved readability.

With clear explanations, practical examples, and a focus on modern CSS capabilities, this book serves as a valuable reference for web developers seeking to expand their styling expertise and apply industry-standard techniques in their projects.

*~Miquill Nyle*